PUBLISHERS NOTES

Disclaimer

This publication is intended to provide helpful and informative material. It is not intended to diagnose, treat, cure, or prevent any health problem or condition, nor is intended to replace the advice of a physician. No action should be taken solely on the contents of this book. Always consult your physician or qualified health-care professional on any matters regarding your health and before adopting any suggestions in this book or drawing inferences from it.

The author and publisher specifically disclaim all responsibility for any liability, loss or risk, personal or otherwise, which is incurred as a consequence, directly or indirectly, from the use or application of any contents of this book.

Any and all product names referenced within this book are the trademarks of their respective owners. None of these owners have sponsored, authorized, endorsed, or approved this book.

Always read all information provided by the manufacturers' product labels before using their products. The author and publisher are not responsible for claims made by manufacturers.

Copyright 2017 InfinitYou

ALL RIGHTS RESERVED

One or more global copyright treaties protect the information in this book. This book is not intended to provide exact details or advice. This book is for informational purposes only. Author reserves the right to make any changes necessary to maintain the integrity of the information held within. This book is not presented as legal or accounting advice. All rights reserved, including the right of reproduction in whole or in part in any form. No parts of this book may be reproduced in any form without written permission of the copyright owner.

Why Meditation Poems?

Juliana Baldec's "Zen Is Like You" is an extremely blissful, mindful, simple, minimalistic, but yet effective and straight forward universal meditation poems known to mankind. The meditation moments are divided into 24 poems and classified from A like Meditation is an awakening to Meditation is like Zen.

Enjoying these rhyming meditation poems can teach many ways to embrace that blissful moment. It can also teach many ways to accept life in general and to manage and overcome negative emotions like fear, anger, jealousy, weakness, regret and any other emotional painful moments.

Reading these blissful rhymes about meditation that go from A to Z teaches many ways how to find inner peace, balance, happiness, inner wealth, aging and growing gracefully and achieving the ultimate freedom and Zen.

Juliana uses the simple form of rhymes to encourage even beginners of meditation to discover their way of Zen in an unorthodox and unconventional way because everyone and even the most busy person can read these easy to consume poems. This interesting and intriguing food for thought touches everyone's life and no matter what one knows already about the fascinating world of meditation.

The book encourages everyone who is interested in meditation to take a peek inside and be inspired by the many ways of meditation. This "Zen Is Like You" book can be used in an unlimited way to help you spiritually grow and enrich yourself - just like the unlimited ways of meditation that you will discover inside!

The one who makes the most creative use of the book is the one who will find the most value in it because there is truly an unlimited amount of applications and uses for this helpful book.

DAILY MEDITATION ETERNITY PRAYER POEM BOOK FOR POSITVE MINDSET, MOTIVATION, HAPPINESS, SUCCESS, HEALTH & RELATIONSHIPS

You could take one poem a day and reflect upon it. You could use a poem and gift it to a loved one. You could use a specific poem to prove a point or to give encouragement, inspiration and motivation to someone you love or yourself.

You could play with the letters. For example, if you like someone whose name is Anna, you could take the first poem called Meditation is Like A and give it to that person to express your gratitude. You can do the same thing with all the letters and gift the poem to someone you like to surprise with a personal name meditation poem. Giving little gratitude gifts like that in order to show one's affection and care for someone is a wonderful way to socialize and to share your own passions for meditation.

You could use the poems for your own daily prayers or prayer books or as an inspiration to write your own inspirational meditation journal.

Some creative crafters are even using them to make their own personal meditation scrapbooking prayer journals, notebooks, calendars, photo journals, quote clipping books, and you name it.

You can do whatever your creative heart desires and as long as you are using the poems only for your own personal usage and joy you can do whatever you like.

Each poem also comes with a quote from professions like writers, authors, saints, poets, philosophers, anthropologists, clergymen

anthropologists, scientists, and more to add some additional food for contemplation.

Poems include quotes by Alan Cohen, Confucius, Buddha, Muhammad, Ravi Zacharias, etc. They are organized by names and from A to Z in coherence with the poems.

The collection of poems includes 24 meditation poems from A to Z with quotes just like this one:

Meditation is like I.

Meditation is great because it is your soul mate and it helps to create your inner peace.

On the other hand, the I of meditation also relates to things like meditation with incense and meditation with isochronic tones.

Isochronic tones and burning incesenses is not really directly connected to inner peace and mental release, but the indirect connection is all that counts to turn meditation into perfection.

So let me tell you this.

If you want to become that angel of reflection make sure to integrate this interconnection because if you don't, belive me, there will be nothing left but a deep deception.

If you don't believe me, here is Saint Isaac of Nineveh's outlook:
"Be at peace with your own soul, then heaven and earth will be at peace with you." - Isaac of Nineveh

The book encourages everyone to start their own journey of enlightenment, introspection, and contemplation and it concludes with some very encouraging thoughts so that everyone can choose to continue his or her path of meditation. The book helps with the discovery phase of meditation and opens the doors for more discovery.

The ultimate goal is to encourage people who read the book to get started and to anticipate their own journey and their own meditation ritual. This is the first and most diffucult step. If you are open and willing to take that first step you will find your Way Of Zen.

Juliana helps with the discovery phase of meditation and with finding one's Way of Zen via the direction of inspirational and motivational poems and quotes so that everyone is enabled to live a life free from negative emotions, fear and painful mental moments.

The book is designed to awaken your own inner spirituality, your own creativity, your own personal individualism, and your own personal expression and to use the book for whatevery your own goal is with meditation.

Turning your discovery of the many ways of meditation that you are brought in touch with inside the book into your own way of Zen is what this journey is all about. Juliana encourages you to discover all the aspects of meditation and tries to connect you with your inner self so that you will find your own direction and your own way of Zen.

Spiritually sustaining yourself and growing into an enlightened and enriched person is only one aspect and benefit of the way of Zen and you will discover many more aspects of meditation as you go through your own journey.

This will be the most unforgettable journey of your life so if you are curious and interested about meditation or if you are already advanced, make sure to broaden your knowledge about many more fascinating ways of meditation. You will for sure get in touch with some intriguing, fascinating and curious ways that you have not yet considered.

Meditation is all about your mind's enlightenment and even if you think you don't have time for spiritual stuff because you are busy or because you just don't believe in it, you will be amazed how different this little and fun meditation book can really be. It will open your eyes and it will open your heart and it will open your mind to the most wonderous and fascinating thing in the world:

Your own life's journey because there is nobody else who will do it for you. You are your own master of creating your own life, your own happiness and your own freedom!

This book is all about yourself and finding your proper path and that is why this book is so fascinating because it is about yourself AKA "The Way Of Your Zen."

It is the perfect little gift that you can give to anyone who you love and it is even a great gift idea for a child who can read because the earlier you start your discovery phase of your inner self the better the quality of your life is going to become in the future. If you love your child, discover the many ways of meditation with him or her because you can not give them a more valuable gift than making them aware of the unlimited possibilities that life with meditation or any sort of introspection, contemplation or prayer can bring.

Make sure to get it today because nothing is more important than your own life and your own destiny and that of your loved ones!

Dedication

For E and my parents who are the most important people in my life!

Thank you for being my angels and thank you for being my inspirational influencers.

You have my unconditional love, always!

Meditation Is Like A

Meditation is like A because meditation is an awakening.
    Meditation can help to free your mind.
    It can help to leave all your stressful life behind!
    Are you ready to explore what meditation could do?
    Are you ready to talk to your inner you?
    And meditation is also like speaking with an angel every day.
    You reach a higher plane in the most wonderful way!
    And always, always remember this:
    "If you want to find God, hang out in the space between your thoughts."
- Alan Cohen

Meditation Is Like B

Meditation is like B because meditation can be achieved with all your brain's cells and the help of some bells.

    They chime and they chime and your inner self swells!

    If you don't believe me here is what Buddha says:

"Meditation brings wisdom; lack of mediation leaves ignorance. Know well what leads you forward and what holds you back, and choose the path that leads to wisdom. - the Buddha

Meditation Is Like C

Meditation is like C because meditation can be quite a challenge and it can be hard to find the time.

When you succeed, however, with meditation you always, always will wind up feeling fine!

If you don't believe me, here is what Confucius says:

"The more man meditates upon good thoughts, the better will be his world and the world at large." - Confucius

Meditation Is Like D

Mediation is like D because meditation is quite like Deepak Chopra.

If you are feeling worn out or down, Deepak Chopra can help you light your way.

He can put you on course to have the most brilliant of days!

Here is what the Dalai Lama has to say to the D of Meditation:

"If a person's basic state of mind is serene and calm, then it is possible for this inner peace to overwhelm a painful physical experience. - The Dalai Lama

Meditation Is Like E

Mediation is like E because meditation puts you in touch with your inner energy and with your eternity.

It fuels your fire and it gives you new depths to see!

Here is what Edgar Caye says to the E of Meditation: "Meditation is listening to the Divine within." - Edgar Cayce

Meditation Is Like F

Meditation also reminds me quite often of the letter F because meditation with fire can help you focus deeper than before.

Meditation is also quite like you're the ocean and you're filled with harmonic motion and the most sincere devotion.

The F of Meditation can also be expressed like Anatole France does it:

"It is by acts and not by ideas that people live." - Anatole France

Meditation Is Like G

The G of Meditation reminds me of meditation with gemstones, meditation for gratitude, meditation for good luck, the Gayatri Mantra and meditation with God!

Meditation with gemstones can bring you not only little but lots of harmony.

Most importantly, meditation with gemstones can help you become whatever you wish to be!

John W. Gardner puts it the following way:

"True happiness involves the full use of one's power and talents." - John W. Gardner

Meditation Is Like H

Meditation is like H because meditation is like harmony.

Meditation is also like healing and like happiness.

Meditation turns all that crazy madness into a wonderful and glorious mental cleanliness.

If you don't believe me here is how Tom Hopkins looks on this:

"Repeat anything often enough and it will start to become you." - Tom Hopkins

Meditation Is Like I

Meditation is like I.

Meditation is great because it is your soul mate and it helps to create your inner peace.

On the other hand, the I of meditation also relates to things like meditation with incense and meditation with isochronic tones.

Isochronic tones and burning incesenses is not really directly connected to inner peace and mental release, but the indirect connection is all that counts to turn meditation into perfection.

So let me tell you this.

If you want to become that angel of reflection make sure to integrate this interconnection because if you don't, belive me, there will be nothing left but a deep deception.

If you don't believe me, here is Saint Isaac of Nineveh's outlook:

"Be at peace with your own soul, then heaven and earth will be at peace with you." - Isaac of Nineveh

Meditation Is Like J

Meditation is like J because meditation with Jesus is something that can help you, too.

He encouraged people to pray and meditate as one of the first things they should do!

Here is how James Allen looks on this:

"Thus meditating you will no longer strive to build yourself up in your prejudices, but, forgetting self, you will remember only that you are seeking the Truth." - James Allen

Meditation Is Like K

Meditation is like Kundalani because meditation through Kundalini can help to clean your spirit today.

Take time to tap into Kundalani and feel your energies flow!

Here are some thoughts about the K of Meditation from Frank Kafka:

"By believing passionately in something that still does not exist, we create it. The nonexistent is whatever we have not sufficiently desired." - Franz Kafka

Meditation Is Like L

If you believe in meditation you know that meditation with lyrics that chant quietly are just great because with them you can really get a chance to change your fate!

Alphonse de Lamartine's thoughts about orators and lyrics are those:

"The people only understand what they can feel; the only orators that can affect them are those who move them" - Alphonse de Lamartine

Meditation Is Like M

Meditation is like M because meditation with mantras is quite fun. Even if it is just for one hour, meditation with mantras can really bring you into that mental upswing.

Before long, you might see yourself sitting full of bliss because, remember this, mantras are always quite fitting.

If you don't believe me listen to Muhammad's voice:

"One hour's meditation on the work of the Creator is better than seventy years of prayer." - Muhammad

Meditation Is Like N

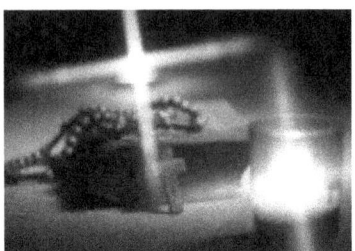

Meditation reminds me quite often of N because there are folks who like to meditate with a necklace that is filled with quite a special power.

They swear on the meditation necklace that is made of crystals and shaped like a flower.

They tell others that this crystal flower can help one mediatate and relax longer and it even makes folks stronger.

It is true and according to Russell M. Nelson:

"Eternal principles that govern happiness apply equally to all." - Russell M. Nelson

Meditation Is Like O

Meditation is classically known with a special chant where you think, say or sing "Ohm."

It's really just a chance for your subconscious to spring forth and come in touch with your inner enlightening judge.

John O'Donohue puts the O of Meditation like this:

"I think the divine is like a huge smile that breaks somewhere in the sea within you, and gradually comes up again." - John O'Donohue

Meditation Is Like P

Meditation is like P because mediation takes different positions. Different positions can lead you to a different state of mind and a different outcome.

No matter what that outcome is because you know an outcome with meditation is going to be awesome!

Go try out random meditation positions because otherwise you don't grow.

Chuck Palahniuk puts the P of meditation this way:

"Find out what you're afraid of and go live there." - Chuck Palahniuk

Meditation Is Like Q

Let me tell you meditation is also like Q because meditation with quartz crystals can enhance your specific mood quite powerfully.

It's like you're feeding your brain with some incredible mind food!

Quarz is also used for watches and it relates to time and what comes to mind is a quote from Edgar Quinet:

"Time is the fairest and toughest judge." - Edgar Quinet

Meditation Is Like R

Mediation is like an R because meditation can also be performed with specific rocks. The rocks can help guide you on your way.

This way you'll know exactly what your subconscious has to say!

The important thing is to try because otherwise you'll end up like described by Francois Rabelais

"I have known many who could not when they would, for they had not done it when they could." - Francois Rabelais

Meditation Is Like S

Meditation is like S and meditation is even better with Sanscrit scripts. Sanscrit scripts and Sanscrit prayers can help you get in touch with your past.

Your past shouldn't define you, but knowing it can help makes the future last.
Which makes me think of a saying of Schiller:
"Mankind is made great or little by its own will." - Friedrich Schiller

Meditation Is Like T

Meditation is like an awful lot like the letter T because meditation also reminds me of Tarot cards.

Tarot cards can bring the supernatural into the meditation thing.

Just remember, however, that the tarot cards are only a powerful tool that is cool, but it is never quite the golden rule.

Mark Twain prefers to simplify with the following saying:

"Age is an issue of mind over matter. If you don't mind, it doesn't matter." - Mark Twain

Meditation Is Like U

Meditation is also like U because meditation is much like the universe.

Meditation with the universe might make you seem very small.

Yet that one little space you take for you is the most important space of all.

Some very lucky few people are able to get in touch with it so make sure you work at it!

The Meditation of U is so true because you do not want to be the one who does not want to find the truth like Leaon Uris expresses it below.

"It is extremely important to know what you don't want to find." - Leon Uris

Meditation Is Like V

Meditation is a lot like V because meditation throughcan help you see how things really can be.

When you understand your world, that's how you can broaden your attention span.

An observation and a phenomenon that adventurers and discoverers like George Vancouver can share:

"Not considering this opening worthy of more attention, I continued our pursuit to the Northwest, being desirous to embrace the advantages of the prevailing breeze." - George Vancouver

Meditation Is Like W

Meditations is like water and meditation with water can help to purify your spirit.

It cleanses you, refreshes you, every time your soul is near and true!

Richard Wagner puts it simply like this:

"Joy is not in things; it is in us." - Richard Wagner

Meditation Is Like X

Mediation XVII helps you realize that you are neither a hopeless island nor part of the hopeful earth because let me tell you it does not really matter where you live because hope does not really exist.

Lu Xun expresses the XVII of Meditation like this:

"Hope cannot be said to exist, nor can it be said not to exist. It is just like roads across the earth. For actually the earth had no roads to begin with, but when many men pass one way, a road is made." - Lu Xun

Meditation Is Like Y

Meditation is like Y because meditation of your heart is really an exploration of your soul.

Without it, you're helpless to go wherever the wind may blow.

A. B. Yehoshua puts this idea like this:

"Traveling is one expression of the desire to cross boundaries." - B. Yehoshua

Meditation Is Like Z

Lastly, meditation is like Z because meditation is zen.

This zen can finally bring you some peace.

It may be the final step to help you finally release.

This Z of Meditation reminds me of Ravi Zacharias who says:

"No matter how much we try to run away from this thirst for the answer to life, for the meaning of life, the intensity only gets stronger and stronger. We cannot escape these spiritual hungers." - Ravi Zacharias

Conclusion

Meditation every day can help you change your life.
    It can be the tool that is needed to eliminate your life's strife.
    A few minutes is all it takes to explore your inner self.
    Practicing that every day is guaranteed to bring to you that enlightened pray.

Final Words & Your Own Spiritual Journey Begins Now

Zen is your own manifestation and Zen is what you take with you every step you make and wherever you go.

Zen is universal and Zen is everywhere.

Zen is like a shadow that silently follows you.

Zen is nothingness, on one hand, but on the other hand it is what makes you you.

The objective of Zen is therefore staying true to you.

To reach your Zen do everything you can: manifest, keep and maintain a daily ritual that keeps you balanced and on the right way.

The goal of this daily ritual is to find your way of enlightenment, your way of happiness, your way of inner peace, your way of mindfulness and bliss, your balance of ying and yang and your way of the ultimate truth.

Never forget about the mind body connection because this is how you will ultimately find your true way of Zen.

Only by understanding and living that mind body connection will you be able to ultimately live your life in the Zen way.

Lastly, never, never forget your life is yours to live and your mind is yours to be mindful with. It is always you who chooses to live and think, or to think and live because only you can manifest your life and your body and your mind. When you do not choose to think about how you intend to live, or when you do not choose to live it like you think, it lives and it thinks you. Never ever let that happen to you!

When you manifest and occupy your mind and your body and when you consciously choose to live and think your life, you will be enabled to lead a happy life and a deep spirituality and this is how you will reach your way of Zen like a very wise man!

And always, always remember these words of the ultimate Zen truth if you find yourself on the wrong way...

"You cannot travel the path until you have become the path itself"- Buddha

Did you love *Daily Meditation Eternity Prayer Poem Book For Positve Mindset, Motivation, Happiness, Success, Health & Relationships*? Then you should read *Daily Meditation Beginner's Guide From Happines & Good Life to Stress Release, Relaxation, Healing, Weight Loss & Zen* by Juliana Baltimoore!

InfinitYou's Daily Meditation Beginner's Guide From Happines & Good Life toStress Release, Relaxation, Healing, Weight Loss & Zen combines soul & spirit searching, flexibility & the modern lifestyle, and powerful meditation techniques in a very strategical and unique way and creates the ultimate effortless system for everybody who wants to enjoy a life with meditation. This book has been created for beginners and advanced users alike and it is perfect for people who have tried to integrate meditation into their life but have failed because of time constraints and modern life complexities. The book reveals the latest insights into the mind-body consciousness connection and how to make meditation work in todays world where time has become such a valuable resource. Especially watch out for the secret success ingredient that is going to be the connecting part and the reason why her system works so well for people who always lack time. This secret technique makes this system work for everyone who would love to enjoy a lifestyle with meditation. Many people who would love to lead a lifestyle with meditation are unable to go through with it because they don't have enough time and therefore think meditation is not for them and then they give up. This system closes the gap and resolves this problem forever and helps you to achieve a proper daily meditation ritual that is real. Heck, you can do this. The key here is to give this system a chance and learn how to benefit from this secret success ingredient. Why? Because it is easy to do and it is effortless to do and best of all it only takes 5 minutes to do. Everyone who really wants to achieve a true meditation lifestyle is able to apply this and there are no excuses why you can't do it. It takes no effort and time at all! Heck you can even do this if you have no time for meditation during the day and if you crawl into bed at 2 pm in the morning after a long day of work. No matter what your working hours look like or how constrained your time schedule looks like, Alecandra is going to show you the way out of it and even if it is 2 pm in the morning and you have not had time to do your meditation up to now. This system is for everyone who is looking for a lifestyle with meditation. No matter how much time you got on hand, you can still follow this system and be successful with meditation. Once you follow this extremely easy and effortless system that is for the most extreme cases only going to take 5 minutes per day, you will be able to achieve a proper daily meditation ritual. Being able to apply this daily meditation ritual equals living a lifestyle with meditation which is going to bring you to the ultimate goal itself: unlimited possibilities, happiness, and unlimited health and mental benefits, and so much more... If you would like to enjoy a truly effortlessly system that makes a true meditation lifestyle really possible for you, try this one secret ingredient technique and you will never want to go to the backwards way of doing meditation the old fashioned way. You can follow this meditation system if it is 2 pm in the morning and you have not been able to do your meditation work before bedtime. You might be a busy person and have many time constraints and in this case this system will work wonders for you. If you truly want a life that includes meditation but have not found the right combination that works for you on a daily basis, you must absolutely know about Alecandra's secret ingredient that will give you the 5 minute key to a true meditation lifestyle - a meditation lifestyle that is so valuable and enjoyable to live! Start living a lifestyle with meditation today and if you apply this system your life will benefit from unlimited possibilities on every level of life. See you on the other side where you can transform your lifestyle into a truly stimulating and exciting daily meditation ritual!

Also by Juliana Baltimoore

Meditation Book For Beginners: 15 Daily Strength Training & Home Workout Yoga Routines For Beginning Yogi Students

Daily Meditation Beginner's Guide From Happines & Good Life to Stress Release, Relaxation, Healing, Weight Loss & Zen

Daily Yoga Routine Beginner's Guide For Happiness The Mindful & Healthy Lifestyle With Zen & Spiritual Eternity

Daily Meditation Eternity Prayer Poem Book For Positve Mindset, Motivation, Happiness, Success, Health & Relationships

Superfoods Recipes: Chicken Soup Recipes For Cold Recovery, Healthy Chicken Noodle Soup Recipes, Holistic Healing Chicken Recipes & Homemade Healing Noodle Soup With Chicken

31 Blender & Mixer Smoothie Recipes For Rapid Weight Loss

The Poetry Book For The Paleo Lifestyle

21 Green Fruit And Vegetable Smoothie Snacks: Green Fruit Yogurt Smoothies, Vegan Desserts & Herbal Veggie Bullet Blender Drinks

Blender Cookbook: 60 Blender Cocktails Recipes For Body Cleanse & Detox, Energy, Vitality & Rapid Weight Loss

Fasting Book For Health, Fitness, Weight Loss & Detoxing 11 Juicing For Beginners Recipes With delicious & Healthy Fruit & Vegetable Juices

Juicing Recipes Book For Vitality, Energy, Health And Fitness Nutrition 14 Healthy Clean Eating & Drinking Juice Cleanse Recipes

Smoothie Recipe Book To Gain Energy & Detox 17 Smoothie Bowl Recipes, Cleanse Drinks & Blender Mix Recipes To Feel Stronger

Fitness Cookbook: 60 Healthy Nutrition Blender Recipes, Vegan Gourmet Recipes, Juicing Drinks, Dessert Recipes & Healthy Ice Creams For Wellness, Health & Happiness

Juicing Recipe Book: 27 Epic Juice & Blender Recipes For Health, Detox, Weight Loss, Energy, Strength & Vitality

Scrumptious Paleo Desserts: Low Fat Low Cholesterol Dessert Recipes For A Healthy, Happy, Lean & Clean Eating Lifestyle

Weight Loss Juicing Recipe Book: Epic Juicer Mixer Blender Recipes For Loosing Body Fat, Body Cleansing & Detox

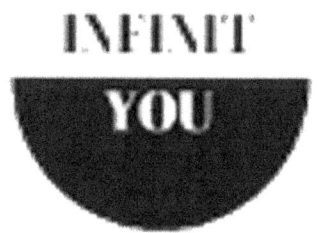

About the Publisher

InfinitYou is a hybrid general interest trade publisher. One of the first of its kind InfinitYou publishes physical books, electronic books, and audiobooks in various genres. Our publications are meant to educate, edify and entertain readers of all walks of life from babies to the elderly. Home to more than twenty imprints such as Infinit Baby, Infinit Kids, Infinit Girl, Infinit Boy, Infinit Coloring, Infinit Swear Words, Infinit Activities, Infinit Productivity, Infinit Cat, Infinit Dog, Infinit Love, Infinit Family, Infinit Survival, Infinit Health, Infinit Beauty, Infinit Spirituality, Infinit Lifestyle, Infinit Wealth, Infinit Romance, and lots more.

www.ingramcontent.com/pod-product-compliance
Lightning Source LLC
LaVergne TN
LVHW012130070526
838202LV00056B/5939